Larry Page and Sergey Brin

The Google Guys

Other titles in the Innovators series include:

INNOVATORS

Larry Page and Sergey Brin

The Google Guys

GAIL B. STEWART

KIDHAVEN PRESS
An imprint of Thomson Gale, a part of The Thomson Corporation

THOMSON
——✦——™
GALE

Detroit • New York • San Francisco • New Haven, Conn. • Waterville, Maine • London

LIBRARY OF CONGRESS CATALOGING-IN-PUBLICATION DATA

Stewart, Gail B.
  Larry Page and Sergey Brin : the Google guys / by Gail B. Stewart.
    p. cm. — (Innovators)
Includes bibliographical references and index.
  ISBN 978-0-7377-3863-6 (hardcover)
  1. Brin, Sergey, 1973—Juvenile literature. 2. Page, Larry, 1973—Juvenile literature. 3. Computer programmers—United States—Biography—Juvenile literature. 4. Internet programming—United States—Juvenile literature. 5. Google (Firm)—Juvenile literature. I. Title.
  QA76.2.A2S74 2007
  005.1092—dc22
  [B]
                                                                          2007022027

ISBN-10: 0-7377-3863-4

CONTENTS

The Google Guys

M any young people today have never known the **Internet** without Google. For millions of Internet users around the world, Google is as much a part of going online as clicking a mouse. Type in a name or a word, press search, and in less than a second, a long list of results pops up.

"I used it to do a report on tornadoes," says Liz, a Minnesota sixth grader. "Google tells you where the best articles and **Web** sites are."[1] Her friend Ginny agrees. "I use it all the time for school, too. And my family is doing a research project on our family tree, and we have found a lot of relatives from other parts of the country by looking on Google."[2]

Google was created in the late 1990s by two young graduate school dropouts, Sergey Brin and Larry Page. Though making money was not at all the purpose of their invention, they have become billionaires many times over. They have grown a little experiment that started as a school project into a company

Larry Page (bottom) and Sergey Brin have fun posing for a photo outside their company headquarters.

that is worth more than $150 billion—more than McDonald's, General Motors, and Disney combined.

Google's purpose—to enable people to have easy access to all information on the Web—is being achieved more than 200 million times each day, in countries all around the world. It is that accomplishment that makes its creators most proud. The story of Larry Page and Sergey Brin is a story about the power of creativity, friendship, and hard work.

CHAPTER 1

Alike and Different

Sergey Brin and Larry Page come from very different backgrounds. They also have very different personalities. But like many inventors and innovators, they share many important similarities, too. These similarities were evident when they were little boys—years before the two young men met each other.

A Beginning in Moscow

Sergey Brin was born on August 21, 1973, in Moscow, Russia. (At that time, Russia was still part of the Soviet Union.) His father, Michael, was a mathematician for the government. His mother, Eugenia, had also studied math, and she worked for the Soviet Oil and Gas Institute. They had friends and a comfortable home, but they were not happy.

The Brins were Jewish, and like all Jews in the Soviet Union, they were discriminated against. Jews were not allowed to study certain subjects—especially science. The government did not want Jews to learn about nuclear power or rockets, for that knowledge could someday be used against the Soviets. As a young man, Michael had dreamed of studying astronomy, but he was prevented from doing so.

The Brins did not want to limit their young son's choices in life. While at a mathematics conference, Michael had met some Americans. They told him about the freedoms that American students had, and Michael became convinced that the United States was the place for his family. They applied for an exit visa that would allow them to leave the Soviet Union, and in 1979 they left their homeland.

Settling In

Helped by an immigrant aid agency, the Brins found a place to live near Washington, D.C. They helped Michael get a teaching job at the University of Maryland, too. Six-year-old Sergey was

Moscow (pictured) was Sergey Brin's birthplace.

placed in a **Montessori school**, which allowed him to learn in his own style, in his own way.

He was quite shy at first and had difficulty learning English —a fact that surprised his mother. "We had been told that children are like sponges," she remembers, "that they immediately

Brin attended a Montessori school like this one, where he was encouraged to work at his own pace.

grasp the language and have no problem, and that wasn't the case."[3] He was teased by some of his classmates, but he loved school anyway. He later credited the Montessori school for letting him move at his own pace, playing with puzzles, maps, and multiplication games.

Brin's most exciting learning tool, however, was the computer his father gave him on his ninth birthday. This was a time when few people owned computers, and a child having access to one was almost unheard of. But he learned its operations amazingly fast. By the time he was in middle school, he and a friend were even writing computer programs together. "We would just sit and play around and program," recalls Brin. "We'd have a program that would talk back to you. We wrote a program to simulate gravity."[4]

The Youngest College Student

Brin finished high school in three years. The work was very easy for him. In his high school yearbook, fellow students compared him to Albert Einstein, the scientific genius. He had lost his shyness, too. His classmates recall that he was very confident about his intellect and even challenged teachers when he thought they were wrong. And while he was never extremely popular in school, Brin says, "I always had friends."[5]

Brin attended the University of Maryland, where he found the work as easy as it had been in high school. In addition to taking lots of courses in mathematics and computer science, he worked at part-time jobs doing research. During one summer job, he helped design a three-dimensional computer program that could be used for student pilots. He was excited by what he could do with computer technology and mathematics.

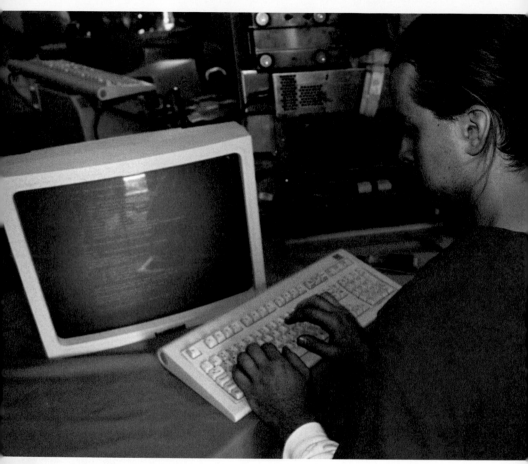

Like this young man, Brin was fascinated by computer technology during his college days.

Graduating with honors at age nineteen, Brin enrolled in the PhD program at Stanford University—one of the top schools in the nation. As a graduate student, he had more freedom to explore his own computer interests, and he was excited about that. He developed athletic interests, too. He learned to sail and rollerblade—and even took trapeze lessons. "I tried so many things in grad school," Brin says. "The more you stumble around, the more likely you are to stumble across something valuable."[6]

Frog and Toad and the Power of Screwdrivers

One of the most valuable Stanford experiences for Brin came in March 1995. It was then that he agreed to take another young mathematics and computer science student on a tour of the school. The student, Larry Page, was interested in coming to Stanford in the fall and wanted to get a firsthand look at the campus.

Like his tour guide, Page came from a mathematical family. Page was born in Lansing, Michigan, on March 26, 1973. His father, Carl, was a pioneer in the field of computer science and taught at the University of Michigan. His mother, too, taught computer science. It did not take his parents long to see that Larry had similar interests. "One of the early things I remember Larry doing," his father later recalled, "was typing [the children's book] *Frog and Toad Together* into his computer, one word at a time, when he was six years old."[7]

Page was also fascinated by how things worked. He soon learned the value of a screwdriver. "My brother taught me how to take things apart," he says, "and I took apart everything in the house. So I just became interested in it, for whatever reason, and so I had lots of ideas

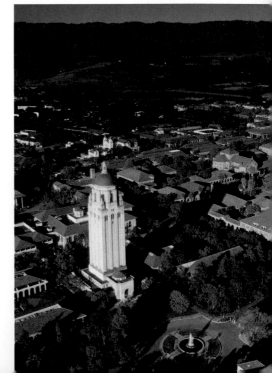

Sergey Brin and Larry Page met at Stanford University (pictured) during graduate school.

about what things could be built and how to build them. I built
. . . an electric go-cart at a pretty early age."[8]

Bright and Quiet

Page tended to be shy but occasionally spoke up in school, especially if he thought a teacher was wrong. In middle school he
had a teacher who often used the phrase, "You can't get tooth-
paste back in the tube"—meaning that it is impossible to undo
some actions. One of Page's friends remembers, "Larry would
explain to her how you actually could do that."[9]

After high school, Page attended the University of Michigan,
where he impressed his professors with his creativity. "Larry
was very different from everybody else at the get-go," one professor recalls. "The projects that he did as a student were always
more ambitious—more visionary—than [those of] all the other
students."[10]

For one of his college projects he built an inkjet printer out
of Lego building blocks. For another project he built a hand-
held computer. "He wanted to do something that was new, that
was different," says one professor, "and he was willing to take
the risks."[11] For Page, however, such projects were just enter-
taining. "Just sort of fun projects," he says. "I like to be able to
do these sorts of things."[12]

Whatever the motivation, Page was held in high regard at
the University of Michigan. His teachers and advisers were sure
that he would achieve great things in graduate school. No one
could have imagined what lay in store for him when he got
there.

CHAPTER 2

Finding a Better Way

When Page and Brin met at Stanford, neither was impressed with the other. Each thought the other to be opinionated and obnoxious. Other graduate students noticed how Brin and Page looked as though they almost enjoyed arguing —each taking a position and defending it—whether or not it was really something he believed in.

"We Are Such Geeks"

It did not take long, however, for the two to gain a healthy respect for one another. Within a short time, they began hanging out together, talking about projects that interested them. They spent so much time together, in fact, fellow students began referring to them by one name: "SergeyandLarry."

One young woman who shared an office with Page and Brin says other students loved coming in to talk about ideas and projects they were working on. It seemed that no matter what time of day, the office was overflowing with graduate students. "I

Brin (left) and Page were both interested in how computers could organize large amounts of information.

remember once at three in the morning on a Saturday night, the office was full," she says. "I remember thinking, 'We are such geeks.' We were all very engaged in what we were doing, and pretty happy."[13]

One project that both Page and Brin were talking about was the role of computers in organizing large amounts of information. "[We] were just doing research in managing large amounts of information, and what's called '**data mining**,' which means finding patterns in them," says Brin. "Eventually we turned to the World Wide Web, which is basically most of human knowledge."[14]

If there was ever a place with huge amounts of information, it was the Web. The two soon realized that the available ways to search the Web were inefficient. And as a result, much of the valuable information on the Web was almost impossible for people to find.

The Trouble with Search Engines

They identified the problem with **search engines**, the programs used by people to locate specific information on the Web. A search engine is important, because people do not always know the specific Web address of a site. They also may not even know whether a Web site exists that might have the information they need. A search engine begins working the second a person

The Google cofounders thought about ways to make search results more useful.

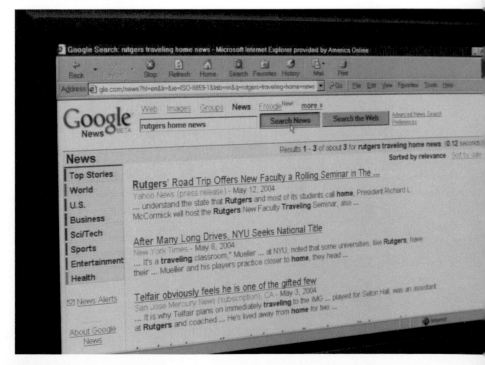

types in a term to be searched. The search engine quickly scans Web sites, looking for that particular term. When it has finished its scan, it shows the user a list of all the Web sites that contain that term.

Page and Brin believed that the search engines were flawed. There was no logic to how the results of a search were displayed. "Search engines didn't really understand the notion of which pages were more important," Page explains. "If you typed 'Stanford,' you got random pages that mentioned Stanford. This obviously wasn't going to work."[15]

What would make more sense, they thought, would be having search results displayed by how relevant or useful they would be to the person doing the search. In the case of Stanford, for example, the Web page for Stanford would certainly be very high on the list of results. How to create a search engine that worked this way would be a tremendous accomplishment— but also a tremendous challenge.

The Magic of Links

At this same time, Page had been working on his own project, looking at **links** on different Web pages. A link is a word or term which, when a person clicks on it, will take the user to a different Web page. People put links on their pages to provide the user with other information that might be useful or interesting.

Page originally had no specific goal in mind with his links project. "I started collecting the links on the Web because an advisor and I decided that would be a good thing to do," he says. "We didn't know exactly what I was going to do with it, but it seemed like no one was really looking at the links on the Web—which pages link to which pages."[16]

But when Brin joined him in the project, they realized that links could be the answer to a better search engine. To them, links were similar to a **bibliography** in a book. Authors are required to show a bibliography listing all books and articles they

Rankings and links were the keys to Google's faster, easier searching ability.

used to write a book. Some books show up time and time again in bibliographies because they are very helpful. The most frequently used links were possibly the most helpful, too.

What if, Brin and Page wondered, a search engine could be devised in a new way—a way that would rank a page in terms of the number of times it is linked by other sites? By considering each link a vote, they could rank results on how many votes each site received from other Web sites. That would mean that the top-ranked results would be the most helpful to users.

A New Search Engine

Brin and Page talked to their faculty advisers about their idea and received enthusiastic responses. They began work on their new search engine in January 1996. They first sent out programs called **spiders**, which continuously crawled through the Web looking for Web pages and downloaded them onto their computer.

The pages then had to be sorted by the number of links they had from other sites. They came up with a special **algorithm**— a complex mathematical formula—for gathering information on the links to which each Web site is linked. The algorithm is huge, with more than 500 million variables in the equation. The result was that for the first time there was a list of Web sites that were the most relevant for the person doing the search.

There were so many pages being copied and indexed, one computer was not nearly enough. In fact, 100 computers were not enough. The computer science department gave them some money to help purchase computers. Brin and Page saved money buying used parts and building their own computers. They eventually strung hundreds of cheap computers together to run the search engine. For a while they used a room in the computer science building. Later they turned Page's dorm room into a computer room, cramming in as many machines as they could, stacked in tall columns.

But they realized that if they were to do a very thorough search of the Web, they would need even more computers. They pooled what money they could borrow from friends. Sometimes they hung around the university loading dock, where truckloads of equipment were delivered. Sometimes the deliveries went unclaimed, says Brin. "We would just borrow a few machines," he says, "figuring if they didn't pick it up right away, they didn't need it so badly."[17]

A Misspelled Name

They also decided that their new search engine needed a name. The trick was to find a name that was appealing but had not already been licensed by another company. It seemed that every one they liked had been taken by someone else. Someone suggested the name **googolplex**, a mathematical term for a huge

Google got its name from the term "googol," a mathematical term for a huge number.

number. Page liked it, but thought just Googol would be better. A **googol** is large, too—a 1 with 100 zeros after it. When they typed the word into a database to see if it was available, they misspelled "googol" as "google." They were pleased to find that google had not yet been taken, and quickly registered the name.

Misspelled or not, the newly named Google was official.

CHAPTER 3

Growing Google

In 1997 Page and Brin decided to make Google available to students and faculty at Stanford. They were especially interested in getting feedback from users. Was the search engine helpful to them? Were people experiencing any problems in using Google? Page and Brin eagerly waited for people's responses.

The reaction of these first users was positive. People loved it and told their friends about it, too. Soon almost everyone on campus was using Google. One professor was impressed with the results he got from searching with Google, saying, "It instantly became my only search engine."[18]

No Luck Selling It

Page and Brin decided that Google was ready to be sold. They hoped that one of the big Internet companies such as AltaVista or Yahoo would be interested in the technology of Google. They figured that $1 million would be a fair price—and that any company that purchased the new search engine would make a

Google was faster and offered more logical search results than other search engines.

great deal of money because it would improve their service so much.

However, they were disappointed. The executives they spoke to were not interested in search engines. They were far more interested in improving the extras that would make their companies more profitable, such as e-mail and expanded advertising. Although they admitted Google was better than their search engines, they did not think it would matter that much to their customers.

Brin and Page had been confident that Google could be sold, but now they were uncertain what they should do. Some advised them to keep running Google themselves while doing their schoolwork. Others suggested they quit school and start their own company. In the end, they decided to put their graduate work on hold. They would run Google as a business—not, as they had been doing, out of their dormitory room, but off campus.

Getting Money

They were lucky that a friend offered them a garage in which they could live and run Google. They did not have to pay rent, and they could use the washer and dryer. But Brin and Page knew that they needed more computers. The size and scope of the Internet was growing rapidly. Web sites were being updated, and new sites were being created. Even though they had thousands of computers running nonstop, Brin and Page needed more computers to keep up.

They met with potential donors, people with money who might be interested in helping Google get off the ground. In August 1998 they got their first investor—a Stanford graduate named Andy Bechtolsheim. He was a computer scientist, too, and he immediately recognized that Google was a great idea. He was also impressed by Brin and Page. He wrote out a check for $100,000. After that, more investors came on board.

Page and Brin set up their business in this garage in Menlo Park, California.

In 1999 Brin and Page used some of the money to move their business from the garage to a small office in Palo Alto, California. Most of it, however, was used to improve their search engine. More and more people were using it. In 1999 Google was handling more than 3 million queries each day, and more people were discovering Google all the time. A few small computer magazines had mentioned the new search engine, and Google's fame spread even further. By 2000 the number of searches per day had exploded to 60 million.

People especially loved how fast the results showed on their screens. Brin and Page wanted to keep the time of the search as close to one second as they could—far faster than any other search engine. Every time they could shave off a quarter of a second or more they were thrilled, for it meant they were getting closer to their goal. But with more searches, and because the Web was expanding so rapidly, more computers and more employees were needed to keep the Google searches fast and complete.

"Don't Be Evil"

Though they had been lucky to have some investors give large amounts of money, they were not sure how Google could ever stand on its own. They did not want to charge people to use it. They had hoped that a big company would want to buy their technology, but so far, no one had. At some point, they would need to find a way for Google to make money, for they could not rely on donors forever.

However, there were limits to what they would do to make money. "We have a mantra: 'Don't be evil,'" says Page, "which is to do the best things we know how to do for our users, for our

Page and Brin did not want to clutter the Google Web site with images and pop-up advertisements.

customers, for everyone."[19] One thing the two had resisted was selling advertising space on its pages. They knew most people hated cluttered Web sites with their pop-up ads and moving images. Besides, they wanted to keep their search results pure—determined by their secret formula for links, not by advertising dollars. If people thought that by typing in "sneakers," for example, the results were Web sites for companies that spent money to be first on the list, they would not trust Google. For Page and Brin, that would be evil.

In 2000 they came up with a solution they thought would work. They would allow companies to bid to have an ad placed on a results page that matched the search. An ad for sneakers could appear on a results page for "basketball" or "tennis" as well as "sneakers." But the ads had very clear rules. No graphics or sound were allowed. No company logos or video ads were permitted, either. If a Google user wanted to find out more, they

Google executives including Page (top) and Brin (bottom) made the cover of *Time* magazine in 2006.

FEBRUARY 20, 2006   www.time.com   AOL Keyword: TIME

WHO'S BEHIND THE CARTOON MAYHEM? ■ BEING OBAMA

TIME

CAN WE TRUST Google WITH OUR SECRETS?

An exclusive inside look at the $100 billion empire that is dominating the Internet

BY ADI IGNATIUS

Google honchos, from top, Larry Page, Eric Schmidt and Sergey Brin

could click on the ad to take them to the business's Web site. But on the Google page, the ad would look just like search results, except that they would be shaded in light blue, not the pure white of the search results. Users would be able to see the difference between sponsored results and the pure results from the Google search.

Soon Google began making money. Companies bid on having their ad first on the pale blue section of each results page. More and more searchers were using Google, and that meant more potential customers. One business that sells men's designer suits found they had ten times as many customers after they bid on a Google ad. "Our business exploded from Google, and Google alone,"[20] says the owner happily. Best of all, Page and Brin had found a way of making money while staying true to their guiding principles.

CHAPTER 4

Challenges Ahead

Google began with just a handful of employees, but as the company grew quickly, so did its need for more people. In 2006 Google had 6,000 employees. Since the beginning, however, Brin and Page have not changed in their thinking that the most creative and loyal workers were the ones who enjoyed coming to work. Making Google a fun place to work has been one of their greatest joys.

The Googleplex

They call their Mountain View, California, headquarters the Googleplex, and first-time visitors are amazed. It is not a typical corporate atmosphere, by any stretch of the imagination. There is no dress code, says one executive, other than "you have to wear something."[21] If someone wants to wear their pajamas and robe, that is okay. Employees can even bring their dogs to work.

Google has a full-time chef who serves three free meals each day for its employees. There are pool tables, shuffleboard courts, and roller hockey tournaments. To keep stress at bay, there are free yoga classes and a full-time masseuse. Many employees say their favorite perk is the unlimited amount of free Ben and Jerry's ice cream.

Not surprisingly, Google is attracting many young, smart computer scientists. Brin and Page get more than 1,000 résumés each day. They say that they hire people not only because they are smart, but because they would fit into Google's unusual environment. "We want people to fit the Google culture," says Brin. "And we have a very open, free atmosphere here, people have lots of fun. They're excited about their work and they work together."[22]

A Google employee relaxes with a game of pool.

Nothing Changes

Google's growth has meant some changes for Brin and Page, too. In 2004 the company went public, which meant that people could buy Google stock. That created a large new source of money, not only for the company, but for Brin and Page as well. In a very short time, both men became billionaires—many times over.

But both men say this has not changed the way they live—at least not too much. "It takes a lot of getting used to," Brin ad-

Google became a publicly traded company in 2004.

mits. "You always hear the phrase, 'Money doesn't buy you happiness.' But I always in the back of my mind figured a lot of money will buy you a little bit of happiness. But it's not really true. I got a new car because the old one's lease expired—nothing terribly fancy."[23] Brin says that he has added a hobby—springboard diving—while Page has become excited about windsurfing. Otherwise, not much about their lifestyles has changed.

He and Page both learned from their parents to be frugal with their money, Brin says, and that has not changed with their sudden wealth. "I still look at prices," he says. "I try to force myself to do this less, not to be so frugal. But I was raised being happy with not so much."[24]

Page agrees, saying that neither one of them began this project for the money. "If we were motivated by money," he says, "we would have sold the company a long time ago and ended up on a beach."[25] One thing they decided on was to stop taking a yearly salary. They are paid only one dollar per year, since they make more than enough money from Google stocks.

Giving Something Back

One thing that their new wealth has allowed them to do is to be generous with their money. Brin gave a large check to the Hebrew Immigrant Aid Society, the organization that helped his family get settled in the United States when they left the Soviet Union. He and Page also set aside $1 billion of Google profits to be used for charities around the world—especially those that deal with environmental issues and poverty.

Brin says that while he has done some charitable giving on his own, he is not as confident in his ability to decide which causes are best. "I am waiting to do the bulk of my [giving] later," he says, "maybe in a few years when I feel I'm more educated. I don't think it's something I have had time to become an expert at."[26]

Page, on the other hand, is far more confident. His biggest cause is renewable energy, and he wants to fund projects that can tackle making gas-burning vehicles more efficient—or in some cases, eliminating them. "When I was at [the University of] Michigan, I tried to get them to build a monorail between central and north campus," he says, "because it is only a two-mile trip, and they have 40 full-sized buses that run back and forth. Two miles! So that's a prime candidate for new transportation."[27]

Headaches

But while deciding how to spend wealth can be fun, Google's amazing success has created some problems, too. One that received a lot of publicity was bringing Google to China. The Chinese government is very repressive. It has strict rules about what its people can and cannot do. In fact, Chinese technicians monitor the Web constantly to make sure that no one reads about democracy or freedom, or anything critical of the government. China wanted to have Google, but they insisted that its results not show such Web sites.

Brin and Page were not sure what to do. They did not want to censor their results. However, they decided that even a censored Google was better than not giving the Chinese people any access to a good search engine, and they did as the Chinese government asked. Brin and Page insisted their decision was not made because of money. But many people were critical, saying that Brin and Page violated their "Don't be evil" motto. And

Google debuted in China in 2006, but the government restricted some of the search results.

months afterward, the two acknowledged that their decision was probably wrong.

Another worry is that the company has grown so large that it has lost its sense of family. The staff in 2006 grew to 6,000 people. Some have never met Brin and Page, although in the past, the two met every new employee. Though the growth has been good for business, it will be a challenge to keep the friendly, playful spirit that Google has had from the beginning.

Google hopes to download and digitize every book ever published.

Looking Ahead

For now, Brin and Page are both excited about the future. They feel very strongly that Google is only the beginning. They have a list of 100 projects that they are thinking about starting. Some of the projects are very far in the future, but some may happen soon.

One idea is downloading every book ever published and allowing people to search the texts online. Another is using the Google search engine to help medical researchers to do special projects. Often, medical research takes a long time because data needs to be indexed, stored, and compared to new data. This takes lots of computer time. If Google were involved, researchers could do their analysis much more quickly.

Larry Page and Sergey Brin have set high goals for Google and for themselves. They are perfectionists, and they want their search engine to make life better for everyone who uses it. "A perfect search engine will process and understand all the information in the world," Brin says. "That is where Google is headed."[28] Those who know Brin and Page say that if anyone can do it, they can.

NOTES

Introduction: The Google Guys

1. Personal interview, Liz, April 2, 2007, Minneapolis, MN.

2. Personal interview, Ginny, April 2, 2007, Minneapolis, MN.

Chapter 1: Alike and Different

3. Quoted in Mark Malseed, "The Story of Sergey Brin," *Moment*. www.momentmag.com/Exclusive/2007/2007–2/2007 02-BrinFeature.html.

4. Quoted in Academy of Achievement, "Sergey Brin & Larry Page." www.achievement.org/autodoc/page/pag0pro-1.

5. Quoted in Academy of Achievement, "Sergey Brin & Larry Page."

6. Quoted in David A. Vise, *The Google Story*. New York: Delacorte, 2005, p. 29.

7. Quoted in Vise, *The Google Story*, p. 24.

8. Quoted in Academy of Achievement, "Sergey Brin & Larry Page."

9. Quoted in Kyle Smith, "$5 Billion Men," *People*, August 23, 2004, p. 77.

10. Quoted in Bryce Hoffman, "Page's U-M Work Hinted at Future," *Detroit News*, July 12, 2006, p. A9.

11. Quoted in Hoffman, "Page's U-M Work Hinted at Future," p. A9.

12. Quoted in Academy of Achievement, "Sergey Brin & Larry Page."

Chapter 2: Finding a Better Way

13. Quoted in Vise, *The Google Story*, p. 33.

14. Quoted in *Biography: The Google Boys*. A&E Television Network, 2004.

15. Quoted in Academy of Achievement, "Sergey Brin & Larry Page."

16. Quoted in Academy of Achievement, "Sergey Brin & Larry Page."

17. Quoted in Vise, *The Google Story*, p. 40.

Chapter 3: Growing Google

18. Quoted in Vise, *The Google Story*, p. 39.

19. Quoted in Will Smale, "Profile: The Google Founders," BBC News, April 30, 2004. http://newsvote.bbc.co.uk/mpapps/pagetools/print/news.bbc.co.uk/1/hi/business/3666241.stm.

20. Quoted in John Markoff and G. Pascal Zachary, "In Searching the Web, Google Finds Riches," *New York Times*, April 13, 2003, p. 31.

Chapter 4: Challenges Ahead

21. Quoted in Adi Ignatius, "In Search of the Real Google," *Time*, February 20, 2006, p. 36.

22. Quoted in *Biography*.

23. Quoted in Adi Ignatius, "Meet the Google Guys," *Time*, February 20, 2006, p. 40.

24. Quoted in Malseed, "The Story of Sergey Brin."

25. Quoted in Ignatius, "Meet the Google Guys," p. 40.

26. Quoted in Malseed, "The Story of Sergey Brin."

27. Quoted in Academy of Achievement, "Sergey Brin & Larry Page."

28. Quoted in Vise, *The Google Story*, p. 68.

GLOSSARY

algorithm: A complex mathematical equation.

bibliography: A list of sources used to write a book or article.

data mining: The process of studying large amounts of information.

googol: A large number, written with a 1 followed by 100 zeros.

googolplex: An almost impossibly huge number.

Internet: The worldwide network of computers.

links: Words on a Web site that, when clicked, can take the user to another Web site.

Montessori school: A type of school that believes in letting children have an active role in determining the rate of their own education.

search engines: Programs used by people to locate specific information on the Web.

spiders: Special programs used in a search engine that find and copy sites throughout the Web and send them back to the home computer to be indexed.

Web: Billions of sites that Internet users share. Sometimes it is referred to as the World Wide Web.

FOR FURTHER EXPLORATION

Book

Casey White, *Sergey Brin and Larry Page: The Founders of Google.* New York: Rosen, 2007. Provides interesting details about search engines and the origins of Google. Good bibliography.

Periodicals

Lev Grossman and Hannah Beech, "Google Under the Gun," *Time*, February 13, 2006.

Keith Hammonds, "How Google Grows . . . and Grows . . . and Grows," *Fast Company*, April 2003. www.fastcompany.com/magazine/69/google.html.

Jennifer Lee, "Postcards from Planet Google," *New York Times*, November 28, 2002.

Steven Levy, "All Eyes on Google," *Newsweek*, March 29, 2004.

Web Sites

Google Corporate Information: Google Milestones (www.google.com/corporate/history.html). This site contains the history of the Google search engine and the company. There are plenty of links to pages that provide more information on some of Google's newer additions and improvements.

Google Fan Logos (www.google.com/customlogos.html). This site has fan-submitted designs, but more interestingly, some of the earliest Google pages and even the logo for BackRub, the name by which the search engine was first known.

Google Holiday Logos (www.google.com/holidaylogos.html). This site has a collection of the various holiday Google logos since 1999—from well-known holidays to the birthdays of Arthur Conan Doyle and Louis Braille.

INDEX

PICTURE CREDITS

Gail B. Stewart is the author of more than 200 books for children and young adults. The parent of three sons, she and her husband live in Minneapolis, Minnesota.